NATURALS

VOL. 1

A PICTORIAL ESSAY OF FILMED FEMALE INTENSITY

CHRIS S. BUCKLEY

ISBN 978-1-955156-62-2 (paperback)
ISBN 978-1-955156-63-9 (hardcover)
ISBN 978-1-955156-64-6 (digital)

Copyright © 2021 by Chris S. Buckley

All rights reserved. No part of this publication may be reproduced, distributed, or transmitted in any form or by any means, including photocopying, recording, or other electronic or mechanical methods without the prior written permission of the publisher. For permission requests, solicit the publisher via the address below.

Rushmore Press LLC
1 800 460 9188
www.rushmorepress.com

Printed in the United States of America

For AM, CC and TM.

PREFACE

In the 1954 drama, "The Barefoot Contessa," Ava Gardner's character, a cabaret dancer, asks a major film studio director, played by Humphrey Bogart, if he can help her get into movies, and maybe to become a star. His response: "If you can act, I can help you. If you can't, nobody can teach you."

With ninety four cinematic credits prior to this film, you'd have to believe that writer/director Joseph L. Mankiewics knew whereof he wrote when he penned the epic line for Bogey to deliver. And a mouthful it is. Acting, like any other art form, requires *natural* ability. Without that ability, no amount of experience, classes, lectures or seminars can make the hopeful performer any more able to achieve his or her goals. I was first made acutely aware of this theatrical factoid when I was one of those hopefuls, with every intention of becoming not just an actor, but a *star*. Acting came naturally to me. It was fun. I could become someone I wasn't. I could over or understate my character, replete with all the little annoying habits of my character, solely dependent on what the scene called for. I assumed that if it's this easy for me, surely *anyone* can do it.

A girl named Michelle (not her real name) would blow my theory clean out of the water, just by virtue of her presence at numerous auditions, to which I'd also been invited. The difference between us being that I was usually cast and she wasn't. Michelle had a single-spaced, two page resume. Theatrically, she'd done every genre from musicals to dramas; attended weekend or week-long seminars, hosted by notable actors, producers and directors, and had seemingly taken every acting class offered on the West Coast. So, with all this experience and training, why then did Michelle consistently stink it up, every time she stepped onto the boards? Put simply, the poor girl just couldn't act. What she could do is *lie*. And that's okay, because, after all, what's an actor, but a professional liar? If they lie successfully, we feel their pain, their joy, their sadness or their anger. Jodie Foster lied to us, while of course being truthful to her character, when she held herself out as Clarice Starling. But it was a lie that I, for one, thoroughly enjoyed believing, as did, I assume, the Academy. In Michelle's case, however, her lying began and ended with the extensive resume. If you're going to less than honestly list "Who's Afraid of Virginia Woolf?" as a theatrical production in which you played a part, *do not* list the character you played as Virginia Woolf. Absent the natural ability so necessary to convince her audience that she wasn't lying to them, poor Michelle never did quit her day job.

Some years later, as a film director, casting several short films and one feature length, all of which I'd written, I found that the unspoken 'natural ability' rule would remain a stubborn reality in cinematic life. Though I was careful not to show it, my heart broke for all those young hopefuls, who, one by one, would step before the camera, and demonstrate their lack or total absence of acting talent. Of the hundreds I auditioned, I found only a smattering of women and maybe five men, possessed of the natural talent so necessary to believably bring to life the characters I'd scripted.

For a theatrical player, to become a character and deliver the scripted lines, while staying *in* character, is generally thought to be sufficient for an acceptable performance. The player glides professionally through their performance, unfettered by distractions or stop-and-start frustrations. Not so for the filmed player. Due to a thing called 'coverage shots,' one scene can be re-shot as many as ten to twenty times, with the player making certain that his or her head is cocked at the same angle for the over-the-shoulder shot as it was for the wide shot. It all gets a bit complicated, but is the way narrative films have been made since the first cameras rolled in the late nineteenth century. It is a special player that can maintain their character throughout all those starts and stops, and *that*, friends, is what we shall address here.

Intensity, as defined in the dictionary, is "the quality of being intense." To take the definition just a tad further, I might add, from a filmmaker's standpoint, "any man, woman or child, in the process of believably portraying a human emotion, such as sadness, anxiety, happiness, anger, fear, remorse, despair, pity or indifference, et al." It is as intense a performance that finds our heroine, via the reaction shot, believably in the throws of silent recognition, as it is when she's choking back tears, while relaying the death of her make-believe mother. Marlon Brando said, in his recorded memoir, [para] "The hardest thing to do, believably, on camera, is nothing at all." Should that nothingness be successfully achieved, it's *intense.*

Why all these intense women? Why no men? Cinema is a male-dominated profession, on both sides of the camera. If you bother to read the names on the title roll at the close of an average mainstream film, you'll find that the masculine names outnumber the feminine by about 20 to 1. With the advent of digital cinema, which leveled the playing field, considerably, between the professional and the non-professional, the number of women, also on both sides of the camera, has risen dramatically. But alas, only the strong survive, and of those survivors, women would appear to remain in the minority. Casting – more about that later – can also be an issue. A woman reaches the peak of her popularity either in her teenage years, her early to late 20s or early 30s. Then, as the years roll by, she's relegated to supporting roles, if any, or back into simple obscurity. While the male star may age gracefully, and in some cases, even looks better, the starlet, due to generations of typecasting and pigeon-holing, takes whatever aging 'mother' or 'grandmother' role comes along. Big money, mainstream studios aim their productions at what is called the "target audience," usually aged 14 to 24. Some studio heads are as young as 21. You can be sure the last thing that 21 year old studio head wants to see is a woman in her 40s, regardless of how popular she once was. Exceptions to this unwritten rule do exist, but are a rarity.

As you may also note during the elongated closing title role, film is a collaborative effort. Everyone, from the dolly grip to the production designer to the director of photography is essential to the believability of the characters and of the unfolding story. Not the least of these essential crew people are those responsible for appropriate hair and makeup. When done right, hair and makeup serve well to enhance or further the character's predicament, not to mention her mood. When done wrong, however, it borders on, and in most cases, enters the realm of the ridiculous. The makeup of today's narrative film, with the exception of extreme cases (vampires, werewolves, gore, et al) is far more subtle than that of yesteryear. Amid the bygone era, an adult female character could be pulled through a knothole, backwards, yet her hair and makeup would somehow remain perfect. It's also fairly common knowledge, as it was in yesteryear, that women don't wear makeup to bed.

While it isn't my intention to give you, the reader, a crash course in filmmaking, something I'm in no way qualified to do, I believe it best to at least familiarize you with, thus, make it easier to understand a few of the many factors that make the following stills possible. That said, the "eyes of the director," a.k.a. the cinematographer, are about as essential as it gets. His or her images are the reason we're here. Every frame of what the good ones shoot would make an equally impressive still photograph. The cinematographer and the director of photography (DP) are not always the same person.

Finally, a brief word about casting, without which we might not be here. Good casting places Margot Kidder in the role of Lois Lane. Bad casting, usually the result of desperation, a limited budget or both, places your host in the role of a drug dealer. Less said, the better. While the director has the final say, a casting director takes a percentage of the actor's pay, or can be paid weekly, at a rate that varies, from $100 to $1000 a day, depending on the size and budget of the production. Good casting is a gift, comparable to the gift of natural acting talent. It's based, in the beginning, solely on what the casting director gathers from their reading of the script.

Here then, in no particular order, as the mechanics of film and all its players remain mercifully un-evolved, are but a few of the images from some of the more intense moments of our very natural players.

Enjoy.

As Claire Bartel, versatile ANNABELLA SCIORRA spends a lot of time on the floor. This is due in no small part to the evildoings of her newborn's nanny-you-love-to-hate, played by Rebecca De Mornay, in "The Hand That Rocks the Cradle." (1992) And no, she's not dead, just intensely in shock.

D: Curtis Hanson
Writer: Amanda Silver
Cinematographer: Robert Elswit
Makeup: Annie Maniscalco
Key Hair Stylist: Nina Paskowitz

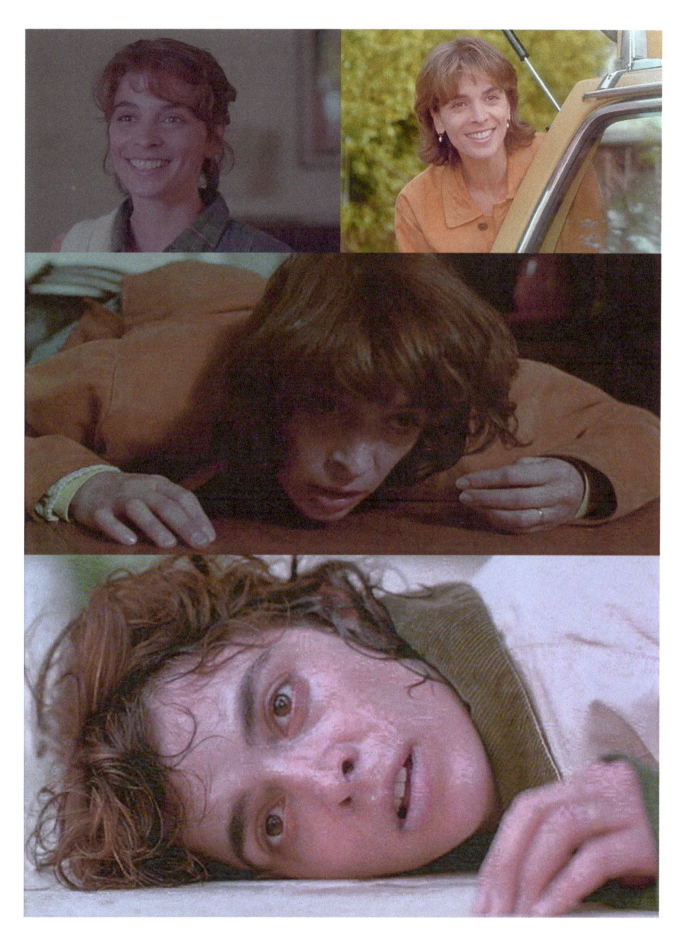

"Ain't I pretty?"

Her character's character. In 1955's "Night of the Hunter," GLORIA CASTILLO's real character, a frightened 13 year old orphan, does her best to convince bad guy Robert Mitchum that she's all grown up, by assuming the persona of someone she's not: a worldly, sexy, and very adult harlot. For one's character to hold itself out as another character, and do it *badly*, is no easy feat, though handled nicely by the very able Ms. Castillo.

D: Charles Laughton
Writer: James Agee
Based on the novel by Davis Grubb

"We think you should apologize."

…was their final suggestion, just prior to blowing up his 18 wheeler. From 1991, SUSAN SARANDON and GEENA DAVIS morph from "Thelma and Louise," the housewife and waitress, respectively, to the same gal-pal duo, though now wanted in three states for murder, armed robbery and assault (of a police officer.) From 1991, a fun time for all. The Golden Globe Best Picture nominee also garnered an Oscar for screenwriter Callie Khouri, and Best Actress nominations for Sarandon and Davis.

D: Ridley Scott
Cinematographer: Adrian Biddle

In the screen adaptation of the play, "A Raison in the Sun," (1961) CLAUDIA MCNEIL is the matriarch who holds her family together, be it with tender or tough love. While her performance would reap a Golden Globe nomination for Best Actress, director Daniel Petrie would take home the Palme de'Or prize from the Cannes Film Festival.

D: Daniel Petrie
Writer: Lorraine Hansberry (play and screenplay)
Director of Photography: Charles Lawton, Jr.
Art Direction: Carl Anderson
Music: Lawrence Rosenthal

The many faces of Idgie Threadgoode

For "Fried Green Tomatoes" (1991), MARY STUART MASTERSON very ably shows us the evolution of her character, who bonds with, then falls irreversibly in love with Mary Louise Parker's Ruth Jamison, circa early 1930s, in small town America.

D: Jon Avnet
Writers: Fannie Flagg and Carol Sobieski (based on the novel by Fannie Flagg)
Director of Photography: Geoffrey Simpson
Music: Thomas Newman
Casting: David Rubin

"Lovelace" (2013) is the true story of four years in the life of Linda (Lovelace) Boreman. From naive, live-at-home nineteen year old, to adult film superstar, AMANDA SEYFRIED quite genuinely portrays the gullible Ms. Boreman, who does eventually get control of her own life. Given all the bad press and political abuse heaped onto the porn industry over the decades, it would've been easy to sabotage or 'camp up' the role. But, between script, direction and Ms. Seyfried's performance, we're shown the sincerest torment of a girl whose only real mistake was trusting the wrong people. And who, among us, hasn't done that?

D: Rob Epstein – Jeffrey Friedman
Writer: Andy Bellin

FAY WRAY, the all-time, undisputed Queen of Scream, as Ann Darrow, can't seem to shake the romantic advances of a pre-code "King Kong" (1933). Asked for her overall opinion of the film, both at the 1934 premiere and several decades later, Ms. Wray stated that her only complaint about it was "All the screaming." When the beautiful, though under-appreciated star passed on, at age 96, the Empire State Building in New York City, where Kong met his demise, dimmed its lights for fifteen minutes, in her honor.

D's: Merian C. Cooper, Ernest B. Schoedsack
Writers: James Creelman, Ruth Rose
Cinematographers: Edward Linden, J.O. Taylor, Vernon Walker, Kenneth Peach
Production Design: Caroll Clark
Casting: Fred Schuessier

Cameras? Did somebody say *cameras*?

Obsessed with fame and youth, GLORIA SWANSON, amid her Oscar winning turn as Norma Desmond, in "Sunset Boulevard" (1950), needs only hear the word cameras to be lured away from the make-up table, and into the waiting arms of the law. Seems she murdered her suitor, William Holden, whose performance also scored a statuette.

Forty five years later, it is Suzanne Stone, played by NICOLE KIDMAN who is fame obsessed, in the fact-based "To Die For" (1995). Kidman's 'Norma Desmond moment' at the mention of cameras precedes this scene, in which the wannabe Barbara Walters bathes in fame, as the cameras roll. Unlike Norma Desmond, Suzanne is acquitted for the murder of her husband, although a much icier fate awaits her. At the hands of David Cronenberg, no less.

REESE WITHERSPOON is a very 90s Gen-Xer who is unwittingly and unwillingly transported, along with her brother, Tobey Maguire, to and into the mythical 1950s TV show, "Pleasantville" (1998). Her perpetual intolerance is eventually softened by her newfound interest in American adult literature. This film worked quite well, though unfortunately, only for those of us who'd actually experienced 50s television, in which the characters, dramatic or comedic, were always caucasian, churchgoing, and never bled (even when shot), had sex or used the bathroom.

Writer/Director: Gary Ross
Cinematographer: John Lindley
Art Direction: Jeannine Oppewall, Jay Hart
Score: Randy Newman

JOBETH WILLIAMS as Diane Freeling, is put through the supernatural wringer in "Poltergeist" (1982). Apparently, the spirits have kidnapped her youngest child. With Oscar nominated visual and sound effects, this horror epic established a few internationally known catch phrases, not the least of which is "They're baa-aack…"

D: Tobe Hooper

Writers: Steven Spielberg, Michael Grais

Visual Effects: Richard Edlund, Michael Wood, Bruce Nicholson

Sound: Stephen Hunter Flick, Richard L. Anderson

Original Score: Jerry Goldsmith

Makeup: Dorothy J. Pearl

AKOSUA BUSIA as Nettie Harris in "The Color Purple" (1985), after a lifetime of abuse, gives her father a pretty good talking to, on behalf of herself and her sister, Celia, around whose life this story, which spans about thirty years, revolves. Based on the novel by Alice Walker, the film was nominated for eleven Oscars and five Golden Globes, taking home three of the latter.

D: Steven Spielberg
Writer: Menno Meyjes
Art Direction/Set Decoration: J. Michael Riva, Bo Welch, Linda DeScenna
Original Score: Quincy Jones

"I wanna kill!"

Such is the heated vow made by PEGGY CUMMINS, as Laurie Starr, in the 1950 cult favorite, "Gun Crazy." Bart Tare, played by John Dall, has two passions: one for guns and one for Laurie Starr. Laurie's passion, however, extends to using those guns on people. Ms. Cummins spoke to numerous adoring crowds, at screenings of this film, as well as her sci-fi hit, "Curse of the Demon," until her passing, at age 92, in 2017.

D: Joseph H. Lewis
Writers: Mcinlay Kantor, Dalton Trumbo (fronted by Millard Kaufman)
Cinematography: Russell Harlan
Music: Victor Young
Production Design: Gordon Wiles

In "Starman" (1984), don't look for KAREN ALLEN to embody the 'hysterical type.' From the moment her character, Jenny Hayden, watches the total re-animation of her dead husband, from DNA in a lock of his hair she'd kept, to her tearful sendoff of that same man whom she's come to know and love again, look for a smooth, occasionally shocked, occasionally emotional rendition by Allen. Jeff Bridges' performance as the Starman was justifiably nominated for an Oscar, while your author was stunned to find no such nomination for Karen Allen's perfectly understated performance throughout.

D: John Carpenter

Writers: Bruce A. Evans, Raynold Gideon

Musical Score: Jack Nitzsche

Cinematography: Donald M. Morgan

Executive Producer: Michael Douglas

Starman Transformation: Rick Baker, Dick Smith, Stan Winston

"In space, no one can hear you scream"

So states the poster for the 1979 sci-fi hit, "Alien," the ultimate blend of science fiction, horror, mystery and suspense. Inspired by – or so believes your scribe – "The Texas Chainsaw Massacre," we find a small group of people (not including the android) on a journey, with SIGOURNEY WEAVER, like Marilyn Burns in 'Chainsaw,' the last woman standing. Ms. Weaver's performance netted her the BAFTA award for Best Newcomer in a Leading Role. She would go on to star in three sequels, the most popular of which is "Aliens" from 1986.

D: Ridley Scott

Writers: Dan O'bannon (story and screenplay), Ronald Shusett (story)

Director of Photography: Derek Vanlint

Special Effects: Nick Allder (supervisor)

"The only thing that separates us from the animals is our ability to accessorize."

So says Olympia Dukakis, as Clairee Belcher, to the amusement of SALLY FIELD's M'Lynn Eatenton, in the nearly all-female dramady, "Steel Magnolias" (1989). Director Herbert Ross presided over a dream team of seasoned female talent that also includes Dolly Parton, Julia Roberts, Shirley MacLain and Daryl Hannah. Ms. Field, who's come a long way since 'The Flying Nun,' is seen here, happy within her character's element, the beauty parlor, then aggrieved and forlorn at the loss of her eldest daughter.

D: Herbert Ross
Writer: Robert Harling (based on his play)
Director of Photography: John A. Alonzo
Casting: Hank McCann

CLORIS LEACHMAN's middle aged Ruth Popper character is a treasure trove of emotions that, until we meet her, has remained mute, aided by a loveless marriage and a decades long dormant sex drive. Just the presence of her boy toy, Sonny Crawford (Timothy Bottoms), however, brings Ruth out of her emotional hibernation, first for the better, then, when he loses interest, for the worse. As for her performance in "The Last Picture Show" from 1971, Ms. Leachman would take home the Supporting Actress Oscar. Shot in effective black and white, this small town Americana masterpiece simply would not have worked, in color.

D: Peter Bogdanovich

Writers: Larry McMurtry (from his novel), Peter Bogdanovich

Director of Photography: Robert Surtees

Casting: Ross Brown

For the role of real-life prostitute and serial killer, Aileen Wuornos, it was necessary for CHARLIZE THERON to, among other things, gain weight. The weight gain, coupled with the efforts of personal makeup artist Toni G, key makeup artist Lee Grimes, and of course, the limitless talents of Ms. Theron, all combine for a spot-on, at times chilling re-creation of the famed killer. Having seen interviews with the actual combative personality, and the numerous accounts of her travails, I can assure you that what we witness in "Monster" (2003) could not be a more realistic portrayal of the facts and the person. For her efforts, Theron took home the Best Actress Oscar and Golden Globe. Kudos also to Christina Ricci on her rendering of Wuornos' lover, Shelby.

Writer/Director: Patty Jenkins
Director of Photography: Steven Bernstein
Casting: Ferne Cassel

She's been a nun, a princess and a chauffer's daughter, to name just a few of the roles successfully affected by legendary stage and screen icon, AUDREY HEPBURN. In "Wait Until Dark" (1967), the dedicated offscreen philanthropist steps into the slippers of blind newlywed, Suzy Hendrix. Unaware that she's about to be terrorized by three men intent on procuring a drug-stuffed rag doll, Suzy, who describes herself as the 'World's champion blind lady,' happily assures husband Efrem Zimbalist Jr. that she'll faithfully, and without a care, await his return from work. It's during his absence, however, that the 'fun' takes place. Based on the play by Frederick Knott, the film, for those who haven't seen it, contains one memorable scene, which can, and probably will lift you out of your seat. And if you're wondering why a blind person would strike a match in a darkened room, trust me, there's a perfectly legitimate reason.

D: Terence Young
Writers: Frederick Knottt (play), Robert Carrington, Jane-Howard Hammerstein
Director of Photography: Charles Lang
Music: Henry Mancini

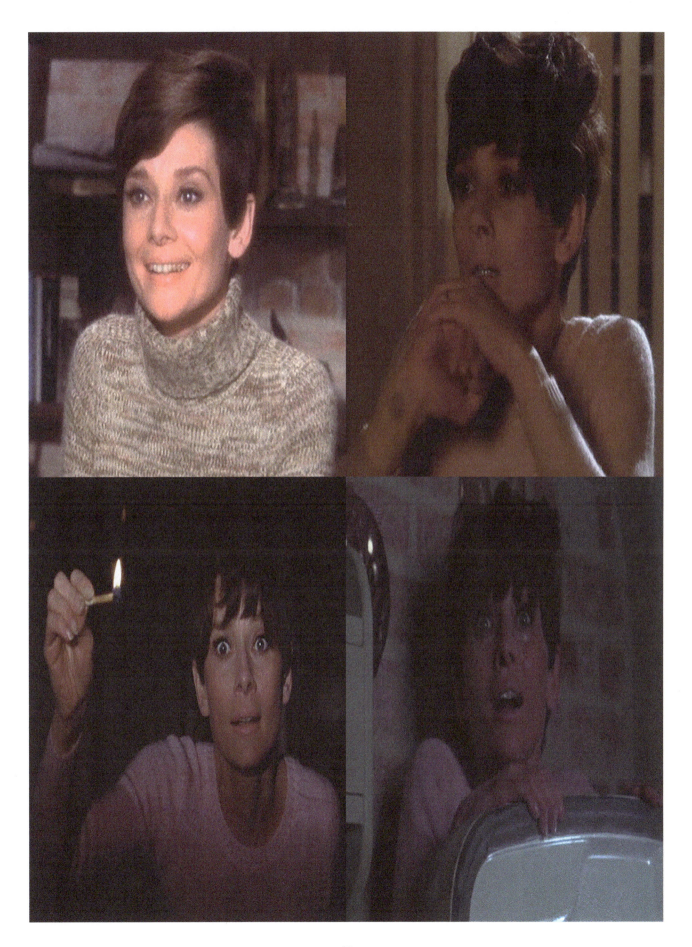

IDA LUPINO's mentally challenged character, Lana Carlsen, after doing everything she can, including, but not limited to the murder of her husband, to land the man of her dreams, Joe Fabrini, played by George Raft, finally implodes on the witness stand, in "They Drive By Night," from 1940. Prior to this endeavor, Ms. Lupino had starred in not less than twenty five features, and would go on to break ground in the lonely arena of female directors, with forty one directorial credits for film and TV.

D: Raoul Walsh
Writers: A.I. Bezzerides (novel), Jerry Wald, Richard Macaulay
Director of Photography: Arthur Edeson

So, you walk into a convenience store, and see this woman behind the counter. Do you question her presence or tell yourself something's amiss? Of course not, she's a perfect fit. A casting coupe. High strung 'Buzzy,' portrayed by HILARY SWANK, who also co-produced, is torn between the needs of her friend and coworker, Duffy (Shawn Hatosy), and her own needs, paramount of which are her sister's doctor bills, that only Buzzy, with her meager, minimum wage job, can pay. Oddly enough, this is only a subplot in the indie sleeper, "11:14" (2003), which recounts five versions of a story, that all lead to one rousing climax. With a cleverly written script by director Greg Marcks, look also for Barbara Hershey and Patrick Swayze, as the parents of a teenage girl (Rachel Leigh Cook) whose mere existence serves to reaffirm the age-old theory that there really is NO accounting for taste.

Writer/Director: Greg Marcks
Director of Photography: Shane Hurlbut
Casting: Felicia Fasano, Mary Vernieu
Music: Clint Mansell

Since the age of 12, JENNY AGUTTER had graced many a screen, big or small, and continues to do so today. Seen here in her late teens, the very capable Ms. Agutter portrays a schoolgirl, who, along with her younger brother (Luc Roeg) and an Aboriginal "Walkabout," played by David Gulpilil, sets out to traverse the beauty and brutality of the Australian Outback. From 1971, the story, based on Donald G. Payne's novel, is brought to the screen by director and director of photography, Nicolas Roeg. Together with camera operator Mike Molloy and special photographer Anthony B. Richmond, Roeg takes us on an Oscar-worthy, at times, staggering photographic tour of the Outback, which is, in this author's assessment, the fourth character in the story. It should be noted, for the unsuspecting first time viewer, that certain scenes are not for the squeamish.

Writer: Edward Bond (screenplay)
Makeup Artist: Linda Richmond
Music: John Barry

SARAH JESSICA PARKER registers joy, disgust, anger and torment, as Ed Wood's real-life girlfriend, Dolores Fuller, in the 1995 biopic, "Ed Wood." As first declared by Siskel and Ebert, this film should be required viewing for every first year film student. Ed Wood is reputed, by those supposedly in the know, to have been the worst filmmaker in the history of cinema, and his feature, "Plan 9 From Outer Space," the worst movie ever made. With all due respect to those 'in the know,' I must disagree. In 1960, a film called "The Cape Canaveral Monsters" would make 'Plan 9' look like a Spielberg Oscar winner.

D: Tim Burton

Writers: Rudolph Grey (book), Scott Alexander, Larry Karaszewski

Cinematography: Stefan Czapsky

Production Design: Tom Duffield

Makeup (Oscar winners): Rick Baker, Ve Neill, Yolanda Toussieng

Young SISSY SPACEK, as Holly, morphs from high school cheerleader to rugged survivalist, in the 1973 fact-based drama, "Badlands." Her mentor, Kit, played by Martin Sheen, would seem to have an unhealthy control of her, as evidenced by her devotion to him, even after he's murdered her father, just prior to the couple's five state killing spree, in the 1950s. This is only one of what would become numerous complex roles taken on quite successfully by the multi-talented Ms. Spacek. Her marriage to art director Jack Fisk, whom she met while shooting this film, would, not unlike her career, endure to this day.

Writer/Director: Terence Malick
Cinematography: Tak Fujimoto, Stevan Larner, Brian Probyn
Music: George Tipton
Casting: Dianne Crittenden

"I'm a girl! A pearl of a girl!"

Having had only one play and no films to her credit, JANET MARGOLIN was awarded the co-lead in director Frank Perry's independently produced drama, "David and Lisa" (1962). Perry obviously had a keen eye for natural talent, which is evident from the first moment we meet Janet's character, Lisa Brandt, beset with what we now know as dissociative identity disorder. Her affliction, which causes her to talk only in rhymes, along with David's deathlike fear of being touched by other people, make for high drama, not soon forgotten. Ms. Margolin's feature film career never amounted to much, though she was often seen in TV guest roles, on up to her unfortunate death from ovarian cancer, at the youthful age of 51.

D: Frank Perry
Writers: Theodore Isaac Rubin, MD (book); Eleanor Perry
Cinematography: Leonard Hirschfield
Music: Mark Lawrence

When Melanie Daniels looked skyward to follow the path of a single crow, until it landed amid a massing flock, I felt her fear. When she slapped the face of woman who accused her of being the evil cause of bird attacks, I felt her anger. As she endured a full-out assault from a group of presumably angry seagulls, until being rendered unconscious, while trapped in an attic, I felt her pain. Such were the travails of TIPPI HEDREN, in the ageless 1963 horror/mystery, "The Birds." Tippi described the week during which her attic attack scene was shot as "The worst week of my life," and went directly from there to the hospital, where she spent the next three days in recovery from physical and emotional exhaustion. Tippi later donated her film script to the Smithsonian's National Museum of American History.

D: Sir Alfred Hitchcock

Writers: Daphne Du Maurier (story by); Evan Hunter

Director of Photography: Robert Burks

Bird Trainer: Ray Berwick

Special Effects: Larry Hampton

Makeup: Virginia Darcy (hair), Howard Smit

INDEX

A
Agutter, Jenny — 46
Allen, Karen — 30

B
Brando, Marlon — 3
Busia, Akosua — 26

C
Castillo, Gloria — 8
Cummins, Peggy — 28

D
Davis, Geena — 10

F
Field, Sally — 34
Foster, Jodie — 2

H
Hepburn, Audrey — 40

K
Kidder, Margot — 5
Kidman, Nicole — 20

L
Leachman, Cloris — 36
Lupino, Ida — 42

M
Margolin, Janet — 52
Masterson, Mary Stuart — 14
McNeil, Claudia — 12

P
Parker, Sarah Jessica — 48

S
Sarandon, Susan — 10
Sciorra, Annabella — 6
Seyfried, Amanda — 16
Spacek, Sissy — 50
Swank, Hilary — 44
Swanson, Gloria — 20

T
Theron, Charlize — 38

W
Weaver, Sigourney — 32
Williams, JoBeth — 24
Witherspoon, Reese — 22
Wray, Fay — 18

CPSIA information can be obtained
at www.ICGtesting.com
Printed in the USA
LVHW071135060721
691956LV00007B/75